THE
Old Photographs
SERIES

OGUNQUIT
BY-THE-SEA

SPARHAWK HALL.

THE
Old Photographs
SERIES

OGUNQUIT
BY-THE-SEA

Compiled by
John D. Bardwell

**ALAN
SUTTON**

BATH • AUGUSTA • RENNES

First published 1994
Copyright © John D. Bardwell, 1994

Published by Alan Sutton, Inc., Augusta, Maine.
Distributed by Berwick Publishing, Inc.,
1 Washington Street, Dover, New Hampshire 03820.
Printed in Great Britain.

ISBN 0 7524 0080 0

OTHER PUBLICATIONS BY JOHN D. BARDWELL

A Diary of the Portsmouth, Kittery and York Electric Railroad (1986)
A History of the Country Club at York, Maine (1988)
The Isles of Shoals: A Visual History (1989)
A History of York Harbor and the York Harbor Reading Room (1993)
Old York Beach (1994)
Old York (1994)

PUBLICATIONS BY JOHN D. BARDWELL
AND RONALD P. BERGERON

Images of a University: A Photographic History of the University of New Hampshire
(1984)
The White Mountains of New Hampshire: A Visual History (1989)
The Lakes Region of New Hampshire: A Visual History (1989)

PUBLICATIONS BY JOHN D. BARDWELL AND PETER A. MOORE

A History of the York Beach Fire Department: 1890-1990 (1990)

Contents

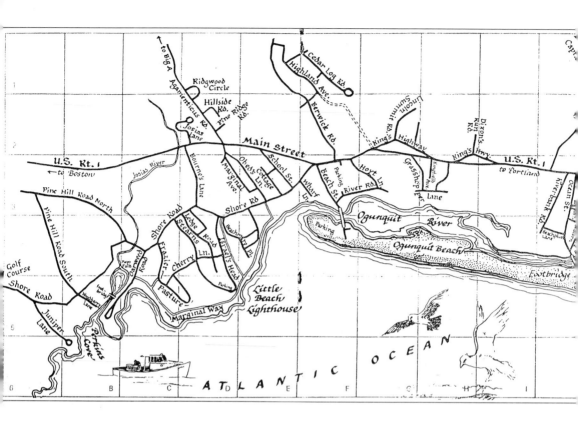

Introduction

The early history of Ogunquit begins in 1641 with a grant of land to Colonel Thomas Gorges from his cousin, Sir Ferdinando Gorges. The grant consisted of 5,000 acres of land on the southeast side of the Ogunquit River and was inherited by his son Thomas. When Thomas died, the property known as "Batcombe" was managed by a younger brother, Ferdinando, who came to Ogunquit for at least a year.

In 1686, Ferdinando Gorges leased 200 acres on the river to John Littlefield (the first white settler), and his son, Josiah, who built a sawmill on the site. Other families who settled in the area were the Jacobs, the Perkinses, the Maxwells, and the Winns. Residents depended on fishing from small skiffs, subsistence farming, and the operation of gristmills for their survival. After the Revolutionary War, local men sailed on deep water ships or plied the coast in smaller vessels carrying fish, ice, cordwood, hay, lumber, and agricultural products.

The arrival of the railroad put an end to Ogunquit's coasting activities but brought vacationers to York Beach and Wells where they could be transported to Ogunquit by carriage. The first arrivals stayed at inns and private homes. In 1888, a bridge was built over the Ogunquit River providing access to the beautiful sandy beach which extended for several miles. Hotels like the Riverside, the Sparhawk and the Highrock were built to cash in on the increasing need for tourist accommodation. Around the turn of the century the fields along the shore began to be laid out as house lots for wealthy visitors who came to Ogunquit to build summer cottages.

The future of Ogunquit was shaped by the arrival of Charles H. Woodbury, Hamilton Easter Field, and Robert Laurent, who led enthusiastic art students to the cove to attend their summer schools. Many of America's outstanding artists summered in Ogunquit during this period— among them were: Walt Kuhn, Elyot Henderson, Henry Strater, Marsden Hartley, Bernard Karfiol, Yasuo Kuniyoshi, Harmon Neill, and Peggy Bacon. The Ogunquit Museum of American Art, founded by Henry Strater in 1952, exhibits the work of those artists that made Ogunquit famous as an art colony. The Ogunquit Art Association, founded in 1928, has a gallery on Route 1 and the Barn Gallery on the Shore Road offers an innovative range of programs and exhibits focusing on contemporary art. The visual arts are flourishing in Ogunquit and artists are everywhere.

Theater got its start when Mr. and Mrs. Edward Hoyt built the Village Studio on Hoyt's Lane where plays, lectures and art exhibits were held each summer for some years. Mr. and Mrs. Walter Hartwig founded the Manhattan Repertoire Company in 1933. They brought famous theatrical personalities to Ogunquit and for five years the performances were given in the Ogunquit Square Theater. The success of their productions led to the construction of a new and larger theater on Route 1 that continues to offer the best in summer theater under the ownership of John Lane.

John D. Bardwell

To the memory of Edward Hipple,
the Ogunquit photographer whose pictures made this book possible.

A Perkins runs the grocery store
A Perkins runs the bank
A Perkins puts the gasoline in everybody's tank
A Perkins sells you magazines
Another sells you fish
You have to go to Perkinses
For anything you wish.
You'll always find a Perkins
Has fingers in your purse
And when I die, I think that I
Will ride a Perkins Hearse.

Written in 1920 by E. Dana Perkins,
an outstanding Ogunquit character.

No doubt there is a lot of truth
In the above little verse,
But it's a good bet that at the end,
Littlefield will drive the hearse.

Written by a descendant of Edmund
Littlefield,
the first permanent white settler of Wells.

One
The Good Old Days
at Perkins Cove

PERKINS COVE IN OGUNQUIT.

THE SHORE ROAD with the Methodist Church steeple in the background.

THE GEORGE ADAMS HOUSE before it was remodeled by Hamilton Easter Field. It could be reached by boat or by wading across at low tide. Adams was a catalyst in the organization of the Cove Fish Company in 1856.

THE JOSIAS RIVER didn't always empty into the outer Cove as it does today; it once veered sharply to the east just beyond the footbridge and emptied into the Atlantic Ocean at Oarweed Cove. Fifteen members of the Cove Fish Company bought twenty-seven shares of stock at $25 per share and used the money to buy most of the land in the Cove and build a canal directly from the Josias River to the outer Cove.

SALT HAY BEING GATHERED ON THE RIVERBANK. The fishermen could row their dories directly into the Cove area and pull them up on the riverbanks. However, the Josias was essentially a tidal river and only a Cove at high tide. Farmers mowed the salt hay on the riverbanks in an area that was later excavated to enlarge the river basin.

THE ENTRANCE TO THE COVE before Hamilton Field's house was built.

CHARLIE ADAMS was overweight but could move in and out of dories with agility. He lived next to the library across from the church. Charlie modeled for the art school students and there is a painting of him with "Bish" Young by Gaston Longchamps in the Hamilton Easter Field Collection.

COVE FISHHOUSES WITH THE BOAT YARD IN THE FOREGROUND. Albert Perkins' home is on the right. People who entered his house had to climb down into the living area because part of his home was underground to help him keep warm in the winter.

WHEN THE TIDE WAS RIGHT fishermen rowed out to the fishing grounds to set their trawl lines. They brought in haddock and cod which had to be gutted and weighed before the fish peddlers arrived.

IF THE TIDE WAS RIGHT the fishermen dug clams, shucked them, and rebaited the trawls with their four or five hundred hooks. They would throw the 1,000-foot lines back into the tub to prepare for another day of fishing.

THE FOOTBRIDGE was planned by Moses L. Staples, owner of the Riverside Hotel, for the convenience of his guests. The Ogunquit Village Corporation replaced it with a foot drawbridge in 1944.

MANY OF THE FISHING DORIES WERE MOORED JUST OUTSIDE THE COVE unless there was a threat of bad weather. They were brought into the Cove for protection when there was enough water in the tidal river to enable them to pass through.

A HARBOR WAS CREATED when the Corporation raised nearly $50,000 to widen the Josias River. They dug out the hay fields on the right and enlarged the harbor by more than a third.

CHARLES MOSES PERKINS (1819–1898). He was part owner of the schooner *Ocean Eagle* and a brother of William Henry Perkins, builder of the famous Ogunquit dories.

ELIAS ALBERT "DEAF AL" PERKINS in front of his home in the Cove. Al had his own boat by the time he was thirteen years old. His shack, built from the timbers of a wrecked ship, was a place where fishermen gathered to talk, repair nets, or cut up bait. Because he was very hard of hearing, he was called "Deaf Al."

LARGER BOATS REQUIRED A LARGER AND DEEPER HARBOR. Government funds were needed to pay for dredging, so Billy Tower, John Jacobs, and Roby Littlefield were chosen to fly to Washington, D.C. and appear before the Senate Appropriations Committee.

THE FOOTBRIDGE WAS REBUILT after dredging made the harbor entrance wider and the yacht basin larger. The unique foot drawbridge was described as the only such bridge in Maine.

JEDEDIAH MOSES PERKINS, a local farmer, sold approximately 5 acres of land to Charles Woodbury in 1896. The property was covered by rocks, brush, and a cornfield. It was reported that Woodbury paid Perkins $400 for the rocky pasture and later sold a painting of the scene for the same amount.

HENRY CARD AT PERKINS COVE. When Woodbury arrived, the Cove was populated by rough fishermen who gathered in the area to tar ropes, bait trawls, clean fish, shuck clams, and wait for the fish peddlers.

FISHING DORIES moored in the river at high tide.

THE BEAUTIFUL OGUNQUIT
SHORELINE provided many
opportunities for imaginative artists.

DAMAGED LOBSTER TRAPS washed up on the rocks and provided yet another subject for the artist.

FEATHERBED LANE was one name for the lane that led into Perkins Cove from the Shore Road. Sometimes called the Cove Road and sometimes Whistling Oyster Lane, it has actually been formally named the Oarweed Cove Road.

WELLINGTON "BISH" YOUNG was one of the fishermen who modeled for the artists. His reported fee was a six-pack an hour!

THE MARSHES AT PERKINS COVE with the Josias River in the foreground, *c.* 1900. Half a dozen fishhouses are between the river and the ocean. The rebuilt Island House is in the upper right and the footbridge is just in front of it.

WHARF LANE led from the Village to this typical fishing shack on the Ogunquit River.

ORIGINALLY, THE WHISTLING OYSTER WAS A TEA ROOM that served tea, cinnamon toast, rum cakes, and the Whistling Oyster mint cup. Helen Ryan operated the tea room and Joy Hawley operated the Christmas Shop. The shop featured long, personalized Christmas stockings which were custom-made by the owners.

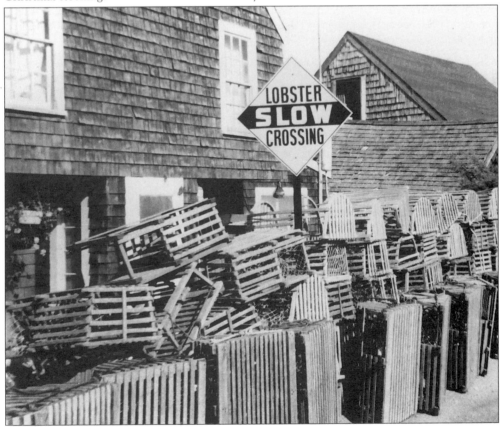

LOBSTER TRAPS AT THE COVE with an appropriate warning sign.

CONSIDERED BY MANY TO BE OGUNQUIT'S OLDEST HOUSE, the main structure was built by John Littlefield in 1730. In 1922, it was moved down Oarweed Cove Road to a site overlooking the basin of the Cove. It later became part of the Whistling Oyster, which then burned in 1976.

THE COVE WAS FIRST DREDGED IN THE 1940s. This photograph shows the dredger at work in 1941.

THE DREDGER CAME TO PERKINS COVE. Perkins Cove was essentially the riverbed of the Josias River and it rose and fell with the tide. In 1927, it was enlarged to create a basin to accommodate the motorized fishing and pleasure boats that were beginning to be used in the area.

THE DREDGER AT WORK. Federal funds were appropriated to dredge the basin and meet the ever-growing demand for moorings. Dredging operations in the 1960s produced gold-rich alluvial gravel and caused a small gold rush at the mouth of the Josias River.

AN ARTIST AT WORK AT THE COVE after dredging enlarged the yacht basin and created a new subject for painters.

THE DEDICATION OF THE NEW HARBOR ON JULY 4, 1941. Maine Senator Owen Brewster had to point out the location of the Josias River after budget-cutting Senator Paul Douglas claimed he couldn't find it on the map of Maine. The Library of Congress and the National Geographic Society couldn't find it for him, either. Brewster persisted and $33,000 was appropriated for the dredging project.

THE WHARVES AND DOCKS AT PERKINS COVE could then accommodate tour boats, sailboats, lobster boats, and other pleasure craft.

AN AERIAL VIEW OF PERKINS COVE showing the channel that was created by damming the Josias River and then digging a trench through the causeway between the point and the island. When the water behind the dam was released, it scoured out the trench with a powerful rush of water. The entrance was deepened even more in 1935/6.

TUNA FISH MIGRATE UP THE EAST COAST DURING THE SPRING AND SUMMER. They used to be hunted by Cove fishermen who harpooned the giant fish to sell to the Japanese market.

STRIKE! The fishermen would hurl the harpoon and set the dart into a fish. The pole then separated from the dart, but the dart was attached to a float which was used to locate the fish once it had expired.

VISITORS USED MANY FORMS OF TRANSPORTATION TO REACH OGUNQUIT but in the 1950s this seaplane fell short of the mark and was badly damaged. However, it did provide an additional attraction for tourists. The aircraft crashed at the mouth of the river and Hutchin's wrecker pulled it up on the rocks ahead of the rising tide.

GERTRUDE FISKE WITH A FRIEND AT OGUNQUIT BEACH.

Two
The Tourists
Discover the Beach

OGUNQUIT BEACH IN 1927.

OGUNQUIT VILLAGE AND BEACH. No one claimed title to Ogunquit Beach for many years and no taxes were paid on the property. One individual acquired a quitclaim deed from the state of Maine and offered to pay taxes to the Town of Wells. Alarmed Ogunquit residents realized that the sale of house lots would restrict public access to the beach and persuaded the legislature to create the Ogunquit Beach District in 1923. Ogunquit was given the right of eminent domain to acquire the beach between the Ogunquit River and the ocean and also the power to tax the property within its limits to pay for the acquisition.

A WOODEN BRIDGE OPENED THE BEACH TO TOURISTS and encouraged development on the spit of land between the Atlantic Ocean and the Ogunquit River. The Ogunquit Casino buildings can be seen at the end of the bridge.

THIS WOODEN BRIDGE WAS BUILT ACROSS THE OGUNQUIT RIVER to provide access to the beach. This photograph dates from c. 1880.

THIS BUILDING ONCE SERVED SUMMER VISITORS with tobacco, candy, and cold drinks. It was replaced by a larger Perkins Pavilion. The Norseman Motor Inn now occupies the site.

THE LAND IN THE OGUNQUIT BEACH DISTRICT was acquired for $45,000, money which was raised by the taxation of Ogunquit property. This popular area has been maintained as a public park.

AN UNKNOWN ARTIST AT THE BEACH.

THE SUMMER OF 1946 AT OGUNQUIT BEACH. Left to right: Mary Claire Kearns, Ann McAfee, Barbara Boston, Jack King, Sheila Lynch, unknown, Eleanor Holzborn, and Vernon Anderson.

THE DUNES AT OGUNQUIT BEACH.

LIFEGUARDS AT THE BEACH. Demonstrating their rescue equipment, the lifeguards are ready to assist bathers who get into trouble while enjoying the surf at the beach.

THE PERKINS PAVILION, where firefighters battled a fire that destroyed the building on March 7, 1941.

THE NORSEMAN MOTOR INN was built on the site of the old pavilion after the stores, the bowling alleys, and the dance hall were destroyed by the fire.

THE ST. ASPINQUID HOTEL ON BEACH STREET was described in a tourist booklet as "offering accommodations decidedly superior to the average." One guest wrote, "I guess this is a good place, we have a nice room, etc. A good set of table girls, too."

IT WAS AN EXPENSIVE HOTEL IN 1915. Rooms were $20 per week without bath and $35 per week with a private bath.

Complete Shore Dinners

Shore No. 1

Lobster Stew
Steamed Clams, Drawn Butter
Fried Clams or Scallops
Whole Boiled Lobster, Boiled or Broiled
Drawn Butter, French Fried Potato
Rolls and Butter
Ice Cream or Sherbet
Coffee

$5.50

Shore No. 2

Lobster Stew or Steamed Clams
Fried Clams or Scallops
Whole Lobster Boiled or Broiled
Drawn Butter, French Fried Potato
Rolls and Butter
Ice Cream or Sherbet
Coffee

$5.25

Shore No. 3

Lobster Stew or Fried Clams
or Steamed Clams, Drawn Butter
Fried Lobster, Cocktail Sauce
French Fried Potato
Rolls and Butter
Ice Cream or Sherbet
Coffee

$4.50

Shore No. 4

Lobster Stew or Steamed Clams
Fried Clams or Scallops
French Fries
Rolls and Butter
Ice Cream or Sherbet
Coffee

$2.85

Shore No. 5

Steamed Clams, Drawn Butter
Cup of Bouillon
New England Clam Chowder
Fried Clams, French Fried Potato
Rolls and Butter
Ice Cream or Sherbet
Coffee

$3.35

Shore No. 6

Lobster Stew or Steamed Clams
Fresh Lobster Salad on Crisp Lettuce
French Fried Potato or Potato Chips
Rolls and Butter
Ice Cream or Sherbet
Coffee

$4.50

Lobster a la Carte

Broiled Hot or Cold Boiled or Baked Stuffed

1¼ lb.	3.75	1½ lb.	4.75

French Fried Potato, Drawn Butter, Hot Rolls

a la Carte

Large Prime Sirloin Steak	4.25
Large Prime Tenderloin Steak	4.50
Large Prime Filet Mignon	4.75
Half Pound Prime Sirloin Steak	3.00

Salads

Fresh Lobster Plate	3.25
Crabmeat Plate	2.95
Tuna Plate	2.25
Chicken and Celery Plate	2.25
Egg Salad Plate	1.75

Desserts and Beverages a la Carte

Jello or Puddings	.25	Sweet Milk	.20
Fresh Fruit Sundaes	.50	Tea	.15
Pies	.30	Skim Milk	.15
Coffee	.15	Buttermilk	.20

DINNER SERVED DAILY and SUNDAY — 5:00 to 8:00 P.M.

Minimum Charge for Room Service 50c

A ST. ASPINQUID MENU. The old hotel building was torn down in the 1960s and replaced with modern motel units.

THE UNITY INN BARN ON THE SHORE ROAD offered the least expensive space for art students, who slept dormitory-style. Before World War I an art student could spend six weeks in Ogunquit for under $100.

THE BEACHMERE WAS BUILT BY CHARLES HOYT and began entertaining guests in the 1890s.

AN OLD WELL NEAR THE BIDE-A-WEE TEA HOUSE on the Shore Road. The large boulder at the turn in the road is still a Shore Road landmark.

THE RIVERSIDE HOTEL ANNEX. Many of the successful hotels bought or built cottages to hold additional guests and to control the real estate adjacent to the hotel property. The original Riverside House was opened in the home of Moses Lyman Staples in the late 1800s. It was one of the first guest houses in Ogunquit.

SPARHAWK HALL WAS BUILT BY NEHEMIAH P.M. JACOBS IN 1897. It was probably named for Nathaniel Sparhawk, the son-in-law of Sir William Pepperrell. The large hotel

burned to the ground in 1899 and was rebuilt in 1903. It had accommodation for 250 guests "of the most fastidious class of patronage."

SPARHAWK HOTEL was torn down in the 1960s and replaced by the Sparhawk Resort.

THE LOOKOUT HOTEL was described in Richardson's 1917 tourist guide as "among those Ogunquit hotels which are universally conceded to be unsurpassed in their special field." Mr. H.L. Merrill was the proprietor. At that time the Lookout had just been enlarged by the addition of thirty guest rooms.

THE LOOKOUT HOTEL ON TOP OF ONTIO HILL had one of the most commanding views in Ogunquit. Merrill made many additions to the hotel between 1910 and 1925. This aerial view shows the entire complex.

THE ONTIO HOTEL, built in the 1890s, shown here on a postcard mailed on July 21, 1923. It was located on Ontio Hill near the Lookout Hotel.

THE ONTIO HOTEL AS IT APPEARED IN 1922. It was considered one of the most expensive and exclusive resorts in Ogunquit. The original four-story wooden structure burned on September 30, 1934.

LOCATED ON ISRAEL'S HEAD ROAD, the Ontio was converted to condominiums in 1984.

AT ONE POINT THE VENERABLE HOTEL WAS CONVERTED TO A MOTOR INN.

THE RIVERSIDE HOTEL was razed in 1973 and Riverside Motel units were built on the site.

DUNELAWN, the residence of George F. Smith, was located off the River Road. It overlooks the river and the beach. Dunelawn was the summer residence for many actresses and actors performing at the Ogunquit Playhouse. It was later converted to condominiums.

The Whistling Oyster
Dinner

Marinated Mushrooms	.75
Green Turtle Soup	.75
Tomato Juice Cocktail	.40
Jumbo Shrimp Cocktail	1.75
Capt. Blight's Delight (served hot or cold)	.50

Filet Mignon	5.75
Lobster Provençale	5.50
Crabmeat Snug Harbor	4.25
Fresh Broiled Swordfish Steak	4.25
Broiled Boneless Sirloin Steak (14 oz.)	6.50
Roast Half Duckling Flambé (boneless)	4.75
Fresh Broiled Filet of Haddock Almondine	3.75
Jumbo Shrimp & Mushrooms (broiled in garlic butter)	4.25

Whistling Oyster Potato
Fresh Buttered Vegetable · Tossed Salad
Hot Rolls & Butter

Fresh Lobster Salad	5.00

Hot Tea or Coffee

A DINNER MENU FROM THE WHISTLING OYSTER, which evolved from a tea room into a fine restaurant. This menu is not dated, but the prices are as interesting as the entrees.

WILLIAM H. PERKINS OPENED ONE OF THE FIRST GUEST HOUSES IN OGUNQUIT and took in guests until 1910. In 1934, the building became a tea room and guest house called Barbara Dean's. It was converted to condominiums in 1986.

SEA CHAMBERS WAS BUILT ON THE SITE OF CAPTAIN CHARLES LITTLEFIELD'S OGUNQUIT HOUSE (also called Littlefield Inn). Sea Chambers was one of the first guest houses in Ogunquit. Prior to that, it was George Jacob's homestead.

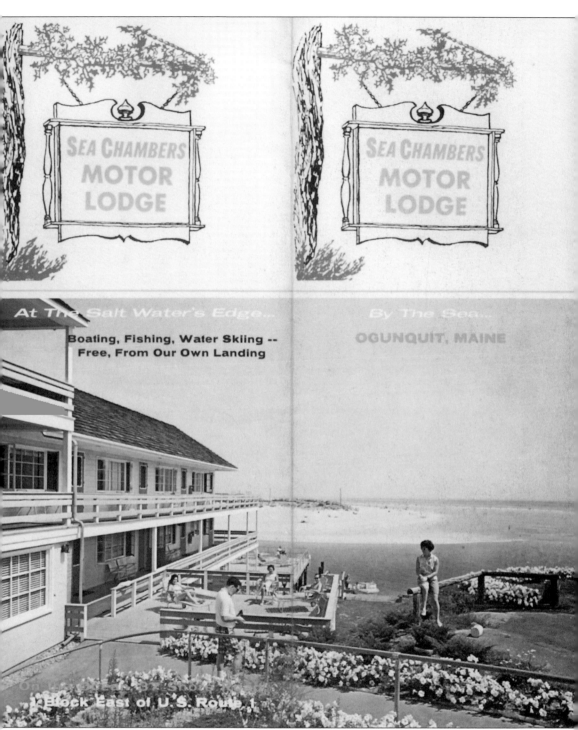

Sea Chambers Motor Lodge

At The Salt Water's Edge...
Boating, Fishing, Water Skiing --
Free, From Our Own Landing

By The Sea...
OGUNQUIT, MAINE

1 Block East of U.S. Route 1

THIS VIEW ATTRACTED CHARLES WOODBURY, who stayed at Littlefield's Ogunquit House.

THE OLD VILLAGE INN was chosen by John Falter as the background for a summer resort scene that he painted for the cover of the *Saturday Evening Post* in 1947. Formerly an old post road inn, it was operated in earlier times by the Barak Maxwell family. At a later date it was called the Fernald Inn.

THE TERRACE has a panoramic view of the shoreline and provides access to the Cove, the beach, and the Marginal Way. The River Cottage, in the foreground, can be reached from a boardwalk.

Poor Richard's Tavern

SHORE ROAD   OGUNQUIT, MAINE

~~~~~~~~~

Clam Chowder   Jellied Consomme
Tomato Juice   Vichysoisse

~~~~~~~~~

Breast of Chicken in Wine   3.75

Roast Leg of Lamb   3.95

Seafood Newburg   3.95

Prime Ribs of Beef, au jus   4.50

Lobster Salad Maison   4.50

~~~~~~~~~

Potato   Salad   Vegetable

~~~~~~~~~

Rum Cake   Home Made Pies
Fruit Sherbet   Ice Cream   Sundaes
Dessert de Jour

~~~~~~~~~

Beverage

POOR RICHARD'S TAVERN WAS LOCATED ON THE SHORE ROAD. The popular restaurant was considered one of the best in the area. This menu was for the c. 1966 season.

On the Southern Coast of Maine   On the Southern Coast of Maine

THE NEW ENGLANDER was formerly the Sparhawk Annex. The name was later changed to Seacastles.

THE DAN SING FAN was one of the tea rooms that flourished as long as Ogunquit remained dry. After shopping in the Cove, ladies could cross the footbridge and climb the hill for lunch and conversation. The building was designed in Oriental style and decorated with Japanese lanterns.

CHARLES HERBERT WOODBURY, the founder of Ogunquit's art colony. He first came to the area when visiting his fiance in York Beach.

Three

The Artists Arrive

A GROUP OF WELL-TO-DO MAIDEN LADIES joined the art colony during the school's first nineteen years. Dressed in long skirts, high-collared blouses, and wide-brimmed straw hats, they were called the "virginal wayfarers" by locals who saw them painting along the Marginal Way.

WOODBURY'S FIRST VIEW OF PERKINS COVE was across a peaceful cow pasture where he watched men fishing from their dories.

A FISHHOUSE ON THE SITE WHERE WOODBURY BUILT HIS STUDIO. In 1896, the Woodburys purchased 5 acres of land off the Shore Road near what is now the Ogunquit Museum of American Art. Charles Woodbury opened his art school in Ogunquit in 1898.

WOODBURY'S ART STUDENTS GOING TO CLASS. He opened the summer school so he could spend more time in Ogunquit. In 1898, he offered a six-week course in painting and drawing nature.

WOODBURY OFFERED TWO LESSONS PER WEEK with a critique on Saturday. The critique took place in the studio or outside on the rocks.

DEMONSTRATING PAINTING TECHNIQUES ON THE BEACH. Sometimes Woodbury would paint a canvas on the spot to prove a point. When he finished, a drawing would be held and the winner left with a Woodbury original.

THE SATURDAY CRITIQUES DREW CROWDS OF STUDENTS. At times seventy-five to one hundred students would gather with their work for his evaluation. Summer residents also gathered to hear his comments.

THE INTERIOR OF CHARLES WOODBURY'S STUDIO. He constructed Ogunquit's first art studio overlooking the Cove in 1896. Eventually a studio was added for his wife, Marcia.

CHARLES WOODBURY PAINTING ON THE BEACH.

WITH HIS SON, DAVID. Charles married Marcia Oakes in 1890. The daughter of a judge from South Berwick, Maine, she had enrolled in one of his early classes. David, their only child, grew up to write over thirty books.

IN HIS STUDIO in the late 1930s. For relaxation Woodbury built model boats and collected stamps, but only when the light was inadequate for painting.

THE WOODBURY HOME IN OGUNQUIT. In 1898, he built a large, wood-shingled home with wide porches. Charles' parents moved in to care for their grandson, David, so Charles and Marcia were free to paint.

AMY CABOT, ONE OF THE "VIRGINAL WAYFARERS," was also one of the "Pine Hill Girls" who lived on Pine Hill Road and came into town on the electric trolley cars.

PAINTER ELINOR EARLE watching as her mother, Mrs. James M. Earle, makes cider.

AN UNKNOWN EARLY OGUNQUIT PAINTER. In 1915, tuition for Woodbury's course was $40. Room and board began at $8 per week at the Hillcrest Inn, the Walnut Grove House, the Ocean View, the Riverside, and Mrs. Daniel Perkins' House.

THE PINE HILL GIRLS were: Charlotte Butler, Amy Cabot, Gertrude Fiske, and Elizabeth Sawtelle. The artist is unidentified.

"THE VIRGINAL WAYFARERS" included the Earle sisters, Susan Ricker Knox, and Grace Morrill. Grace Morrill is best remembered for Stonecrop, her unique studio at the corner of Juniper Lane and Shore Road.

HAMILTON EASTER FIELD, ARTIST AND ART CRITIC. In 1902, Field and Robert Laurent, his young French protégé, came to Perkins Cove in search of a summer home. Field purchased the Adams House, some fish shacks, and a considerable amount of land. Between 1906 and 1908 he purchased most of the remaining fish shacks and land around the Cove. He installed water, electricity, and an icehouse. He also opened a general store where he stocked tobacco and fruit for the locals.

ROBERT LAURENT was about twelve years old when he first came to Ogunquit with Field. Field had lodged at an inn in Brittany that was managed by Laurent's parents. Field recognized the young man's talents and brought the entire family to New York so he could guide the boy's education. Eventually, Field and Laurent built a studio in Perkins Cove. In 1911 they established the Summer School of Graphic Arts.

LAURENT WITH WILLIAM VON SCHLEGELL who taught still life and landscape from 1935 to 1949. Von Schlegell lived with his wife and son in several of the Cove's fish shacks during his summers in Ogunquit. He kept a studio in a separate shack where he could avoid prospective art buyers.

ROBERT LAURENT IN HIS STUDIO at Ker Fravaal, which was named in honor of his mother's family. The studio was located at Laurent's farm on the Logging Road. When Hamilton Field died of pneumonia in 1922, Laurent was named as his sole heir.

A CLASS PICTURE at the Ogunquit School of Painting and Sculpture. This art school flourished in the 1940s and '50s. Students came each summer, some for a week and some for the entire summer.

A CLASS OF PAINTING AND SCULPTURE STUDENTS pictured sometime before World War II. Robert Laurent taught sculpture, Bernard Karfiol and Ernest Fiene taught life classes, and Bill von Schlegell taught landscape.

THE OGUNQUIT SCHOOL OF PAINTING AND SCULPTURE.

A ROOM AT THE SCHOOL in the 1950s. Student accommodations were very basic. Rooms were furnished with one or two small beds, a bureau, and a nightstand.

A GROUP OF ARTISTS. Shown here are, from left to right: Wood Gaylor, Win Gaylor, Robert Laurent, and Yasuo Kuniyoshi. Wood Gaylor, Laurent, and Kuniyoshi were among a group of artists who established the Hamilton Easter Field Foundation in 1929. The foundation was run by artists to help other artists by purchasing their work.

ARTISTS' SHACKS AT PERKINS COVE. Many of the shacks were built by fishermen after the establishment of the Cove Fish Company. Hamilton Field purchased most of the buildings and converted them for use by artists.

RUDOLPH DIRKS WAS AN ARTIST WHO CREATED THE SYNDICATED COMIC STRIP called "The Katzenjammer Kids." He was a man of action who organized clambakes, picnics, and fishing expeditions.

THE DIRKS FAMILY IN 1919. Shown are, from left to right: Helen, Barbara, and Rudy. They had a home behind the present Viking Ice Cream and Candy Store on Route 1. Dirks did not feel comfortable exhibiting his paintings and preferred to give them to people who liked them.

AN EARLY PICTURE OF BATHERS AT NARROW COVE. Note the bathing costumes and the fishing boats moored in the outer harbor.

AT SHAKER POND NEAR ALFRED, MAINE, IN THE EARLY 1920s. Shown are, from left to right: Dorothy Varian, John Laurent, Katherine Schmidt, Yasuo Kuniyoshi, and Robert Laurent.

THE AREA WAS A PERFECT VACATION SPOT for artists and their families who gathered regularly for picnics and parties. Shown are, left to right: Robert Laurent, unknown, Margaret Karfiol, Virginie Karfiol, Mimi Laurent, and George Karfiol.

AN ARTISTS' PICNIC at Bauneg Beg, near Alfred, ME included, from left to right: Lili Meillard, Bae von Schlegell, Mimi Laurent, Robert Laurent, John Laurent, and the Italian artist Ludivicco.

THE KARFIOL FAMILY at their Pine Hill Road cottage that was built in 1925. Bernard Karfiol taught life classes at the art school.

MIMI LAURENT WITH HER SONS JOHN AND PAUL IN 1933.

THIS FOURSOME PLAYED GOLF REGULARLY and the players were serious about their scores. From 1937 to 1947 they held the Big Boy Golf Tournament for artists. (A sketch on a scrap of paper could qualify a friend as an artist.) Pictured are, from left to right: Robert Laurent, Cliff Sterrett, Rudy Dirks, and Richard Lahey.

A GROUP OF GOLFERS, c. 1937. From left to right: Max von Schlegell (David's favorite uncle), Rudy Dirks, Robert Laurent, and Richard Lahey.

WALT KUHN AND HIS DAUGHTER BRENDA. Walt's first visit to Ogunquit was in 1911, but it wasn't until 1920 that he became a regular summer visitor. He was easily one of the most influential artists to have lived here.

WALT KUHN AND HIS WIFE VERA on the porch of the Sterns Road cottage where Walt spent most of his summers until just before his death in 1949.

RUDY DIRKS, WALT KUHN, AND AL FRUEH, *c.* 1925. Kuhn was one of four men who organized the 1913 Armory Show of modern art in New York City. It has been called the most influential exhibition ever held in America.

WALT AND VERA KUHN IN THEIR CONVERTIBLE.

CHANNING HARE'S PAINTING OF BEATRICE LILLY. Channing Hare was a brilliant society portrait painter who commanded top prices for his work. However, he devoted much of his energy to gathering interesting people for elaborate cocktail parties and for late-night theater parties thrown to celebrate the opening of each new show at the Playhouse.

MOUNTFORT COOLIDGE managed the Hare and Coolidge Antique Shop after World War II. Coolidge, a student of Hamilton Field, came to Ogunquit as early as 1917 and spent his time painting for shows or working in the antique shop that he opened with Hare in 1920.

PARTIES WERE SPONTANEOUS
and the old icehouse building was a
popular location.

THE LAURENTS OFTEN INVITED YOUNG ARTISTS to share the rich cultural
surroundings of their own art collection. Pictured are, from left to right: Gaston and Weeda
Longchamps, Paul Laurent, Lili Meillard, Mimi, John and Robert Laurent, and Janette and
Ernest Fiene.

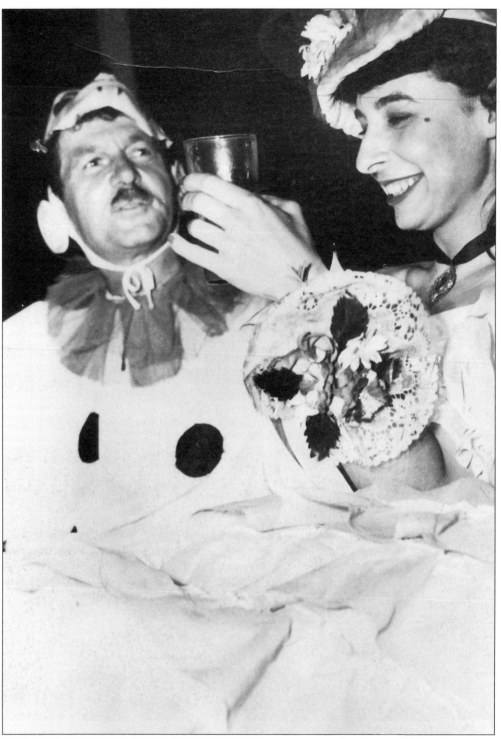

THE ARTISTS' BALLS HELD AT THE COVE became so popular that they had to be moved to larger facilities such as the Cliff Country Club and the York Beach Casino. Robert Laurent and Mitzi Soloman are shown here in costume in the 1940s.

THEY DANCED UNTIL DAWN while the townspeople gathered to see their costumes. Brawls would sometimes break out between party-goers and onlookers. Such conflicts grew more and more frequent and the the Artists' Balls were ended in 1952.

AN EARLY ARTISTS' BALL. These annual costume parties were sponsored by the art school to raise tuition money for talented students with limited resources. They were held at the end of the season and everyone was welcome. Costumes were required and artists, students, summer residents, and members of the theater colony used great imagination in designing them.

LARGE PARTIES AT THE ICEHOUSE BECAME POPULAR IN THE 1950s. Mike Horn is on the clarinet with a jazz band made up of artists and summer friends.

THE BAND included Hal Carney on bass, John Laurent on guitar, Paul Laurent on accordion, Mike Horn on clarinet, Louis Benoit or Jack Smart on drums, and an occasional extra.

BILLY TOWER AND LEON PERKINS
with a giant tuna that they brought into
the Cove.

GEORGE WEARE AND HENRY STRATER introduced sport fishing for tuna with a rod and
reel. It wasn't unusual to see large catches of tuna hanging at the town dock in the Cove. From
left to right: Ray Shum, George Weare, Cliff North, Rudy Dirks, and Henry Strater.

The OGUNQUIT ART CENTER

SEVENTEENTH ANNUAL EXHIBITION

PAINTINGS, ETCHINGS, SCULPTURES

N. VAYANA, Director

IN SUMMERTIME   BY E. DUFNER

JULY 3 to SEPTEMBER 5, 1939

HOYT'S LANE   -:-   OGUNQUIT, MAINE

NUNZIO VAYANA'S OGUNQUIT ART CENTER opened in 1922. It was the community's first commercial art gallery and both professionals and amateurs were encouraged to exhibit there. Two exhibitions were held each summer.

ISABEL LEWANDO AT THE COVE. She remained in the area and became a talented photographer.

ELYOT HENDERSON, a former pupil of Laurent and von Schlegell, became an early member of the Ogunquit Art Association and encouraged the Laurent group to become involved in its organization. Henderson painted oil portraits of models and of local residents.

MANY OF THE ARTISTS OPENED SHOPS OR GALLERIES and survived on purchases by local patrons. Some artists held regular "clothesline sales" to promote the sale of their work.

THE SUNRISE STUDIO IN 1922. German-born artist Fritz Richter served as president of the Ogunquit Art Association for ten years and gave encouragement to the artists from his base at the old Sunrise Studio.

NED HERGELROTH AT HIS EASEL.
Hergelroth became an accomplished
painter of the ocean and the rocky
shoreline. In the winters he served as
chairman of the Art Education
Department at Temple University's Tyler
School of Art.

DAVID VON SCHLEGELL AND ONE OF
HIS EARLY SCULPTURES. The only child
of Bae and William von Schlegell, David
experimented with scenes of rocks and boats,
expressionist drawings, distorted figure
paintings, and abstract landscapes before
turning to sculpture in the 1960s.

A 1923 COVER FOR *SKETCH* MAGAZINE BY HARMON NEILL. Neill was an illustrator who contributed to numerous magazines. For several seasons he published *The Sketch*, a weekly news magazine about the latest social and artistic events.

HARMON NEILL FIRST CAME TO OGUNQUIT IN 1922. He was a portrait artist and a friend of Walt Kuhn. Neill became a permanent resident in the 1940s and lived in Ogunquit with his family until his death in 1981.

DEWITT HARDY once worked as a framer in Chris Ritter's gallery. He later became curator and then associate director of the Museum of Art of Ogunquit, and a nationally recognized artist.

PAT SCHLOZ HARDY WITH HER TWIN SONS. Pat also pursued her art career in the area. The Hardys eventually moved to North Berwick when owning real estate in Ogunquit became unrealistic.

ROBERT LAURENT DONATED THE HAMILTON EASTER FIELD ART FOUNDA-
TION COLLECTION to the Barn Gallery Associates in 1966. Generous donations provided
funds for a special room to house the collection.

ELYOT HENDERSON AND HARMON NEILL IN 1967.

HENRY STRATER'S FAMOUS SILHOUETTE in the doorway of the Ogunquit Art Museum.

HENRY STRATER BOUGHT WOODBURY'S MEADOW overlooking Narrow Cove in 1951. He formed a non-profit corporation called the Museum of Art of Ogunquit. The corporation built a gallery here which opened for its first exhibition in 1953.

THE OGUNQUIT ART ASSOCIATION MOVED INTO A YELLOW BARN at the Ogunquit House on the Shore Road in 1936. It was later converted to offices for the Sea Chambers resort complex.

A LARGE NEW GALLERY AND EDUCATION COMPLEX was proposed in 1958. The response to a request for financial support was overwhelming and the first phase of the Barn Gallery was completed within a year. Most of the exhibition space was leased to the Ogunquit Art Association and a summer art education program was launched.

THE COVE STUDIO WAS BEVERLY HALLAM'S GALLERY IN PERKINS COVE. Hallam began spending summers in Ogunquit in 1949 and is credited with introducing acrylic to local artists.

THE FORMER SCHOOL OF PAINTING AND SCULPTURE BUILDING is shown here as a gift shop and gallery in 1984.

THE INCOMPARABLE TALLULAH BANKHEAD promoting her appearance in *Dear Charles*. She was featured in several Playhouse productions including *Her Cardboard Lover* in 1941.

Four
The Actresses and Actors Arrive

WALTER HARTWIG, A FORMER HOLLYWOOD DIRECTOR AND BROADWAY PRODUCER, participated in play readings at this art center on Hoyt's Lane. In 1932 he leased Mrs. Moses Perkins' garage on the Shore Road and converted it to a theater. The company operated there from 1933 to 1936.

AFTER THE 1936 SEASON Hartwig purchased part of the Weare farm on Route 1 and engaged theater architect Alexander Wychoff to design a new building. The new theater opened on July 19, 1939, with *Boy Meets Girl*. Tickets ranged in price from 75¢ to $2.

EDWARD EVERETT HORTON FIRST APPEARED IN OGUNQUIT IN 1939 when he performed in his perennial vehicle *Springtime for Henry*. Walter Hartwig died in January 1941 and his widow, Maude Hartwig, took over the operation of the theater. She brought New York's most distinguished playwright/producer, George Abbott, to Ogunquit to share the managerial responsibilities.

THE PLAYHOUSE LOBBY IN 1963.

BETSY PALMER, one of
television's most talented and
sparkling personalities, has
appeared in ten productions at the
Playhouse.

SHIRLEY BOOTH appeared in *The
Late Christopher Bean* in the summer of
1960.

GARY MERRILL IN REHEARSAL. Ogunquit's resident company was one of the best. Top stars flocked to the small village, rehearsed with the resident company, and brought splendid theater to the summer colony.

JESSICA TANDY AND HUME CRONYN were among the top stars that came to Ogunquit to perform at the Playhouse.

IN 1951 JOHN LANE ACQUIRED THE GROUNDS AND BUILDING FROM MAUDE HARTWIG. His first problem was replacing the stage end of the theater which had been damaged in a November 1950 hurricane.

LANE TURNED THE FRONT PARKING LOT INTO LAWNS AND GARDENS, added new lighting equipment, and installed air conditioning and heating. Later, he installed new seats and built an orchestra pit.

RUDY VALLEE ON STAGE. The stage at the Playhouse was larger than many Broadway playhouses. The auditorium seated seven hundred people and the building had the most modern technical facilities available at the time.

FRANK FONTAINE, who became famous on the Jackie Gleason television show, posing with Charlie Ganellas, owner of Valeries, in front of the Ogunquit Spring Water sign. The young people in the picture are a few of Frankie's children. He was noted for having a very large family.

CLAUDETTE COLBERT ON STAGE. By the late 1950s, the resident company was gone. Stars rehearsed in New York with one company and traveled from theater to theater together.

AN AERIAL VIEW OF THE SQUARE with Jacobs' garage in the center and Valerie's directly across the street. The sign on the garage enabled pilots flying over the area to be sure of their location.

Five
Ogunquit Village

THE STREETCAR CAME TO OGUNQUIT around the turn of the century and at the same time electricity became widely available. Attempts to get funding for street lights were rejected at a Wells town meeting. Angry Ogunquit voters went to the state legislature in 1913 and got a charter for the Ogunquit Village Corporation. In 1914, at the first regular meeting of the Corporation, $350 was voted for street lights.

THE SHORE ROAD near the junction of Wharf Lane in 1890. The wagon tracks lead down the Shore Road towards Perkins Lane.

THE SHORE ROAD winds its way along the edge of the ocean between Ogunquit Village and York Beach.

THE MARGINAL WAY. In 1925, at the annual meeting of the Village Corporation, a vote of thanks was given to Josiah Chase for his gift of the "Marginal Way" to the people of Ogunquit. It was one of the finest gifts that the Village would ever receive.

RIVER ROAD provided the opportunity for a scenic ride along the banks of the Ogunquit River.

THIS POSTER ANNOUNCED THE DEDICATION OF THE MARGINAL WAY IN 1946. Everyone was invited.

THE DEDICATION OF THE MARGINAL WAY on August 12, 1946. A large crowd gathered to hear the speakers and show their appreciation for this wonderful gift to the Village.

THE MARGINAL WAY. This view of the seashore from the Marginal Way shows why tourists and artists have been so attracted to the area.

AN EARLY VIEW OF THE INTERSECTION OF BEACH STREET AND SHORE ROAD.

OGUNQUIT SQUARE LOOKING NORTH IN 1885. Andrew's grocery store is on the left. In the right background is Barak Maxwell's house, once a post road inn, now the Old Village Inn. In the foreground is the intersection of Route 1 and Beach Street.

THE STONE LIBRARY IS ON THE LEFT AND THE BAPTIST CHURCH IS ON THE RIGHT in this picture of the Shore Road looking toward the center of the Village. Note the granite posts linked by chains in front of the library building. The Memorial Library was given to the Village by Mrs. George Conarroe in 1897.

A VIEW TOWARD MAIN STREET FROM THE SHORE ROAD IN THE EARLY 1900s. The trolley car tracks on the left help date this picture.

DR. GORDON'S PHARMACY AFTER 1900. It was razed to widen the entrance to Beach Street.

MAIN STREET LOOKING NORTH UP SCOTCH HILL. On the left, across Berwick Road, was the Rockland Hotel, later called the Maxwell House.

THE LOCAL MEN'S CLUB PROMISED A MINUTE OF PEACE WITH NO PHONE INTERRUPTIONS. Shown here are, from right to left: Arthur Perkins, Roby Littlefield, J.P. Littlefield, George Ramsdell, ? Goodwin, Walter Hatch, Fred Kemp, Harley Freeman, Jerry Handspicker, Frank Hatch, Orison Perkins, Fred Kemp, Jr., Edson Mayo, Willis Littlefield, and Horace ? .

THE ANNUAL PERKINS COVE LOBSTER BAKE was sponsored by the Ogunquit Resort Association and the Civic Club. Shown enjoying it are, from left to right: Russell Ireland, Lawrence Fernald, Roby Littlefield, Kenny Young, Harold Rowe, Billy Tower, Senator James Erwin, and Anne Erwin.

THE OGUNQUIT BAPTIST CHURCH CHOIR in the early 1940s. From left right: (front row) Charlotte Allen, Penny Powers, Nancy Littlefield, Miriam Littlefield, Marion Adams, and Katie Boston; (second row) Evelyn Moulton, Norma Littlefield, and Margaret Cady; (third row) Roberta Staples, Carolyn Robinson, Teddy Eaton, Mary Henderson, Pat Fortuine, and Elizabeth Moulton; (back row) pianist Frances McAfee, Jane Bernard, Phyllis Bradshaw, Eleanor Hayes, and Choir Director Amanda Littlefield.

GRADES ONE AND TWO AT THE GRAMMAR SCHOOL IN THE 1930s. Left to right: (front row) Richard Ramsdell, Paul Perkins, Lloyd Moulton, Gordon Perkins, Paul Varney, Benjamin Davis, Arthur Hayes, Earl Young, and Carroll Kemp; (middle row) Joe Littlefield, John Jacobs, Jeff Powers, Laighton Lord, Maynard Fernald, Gordon Johnson, Barbara Gleason, Mildred Young, Primrose Littlefield, and Doris Smith; (back row) Kenneth Ramsdell, Mae Winn, Barbara Nadeau, Eunice Littlefield, Hazel Weare, Elizabeth Littlefield, Marguerite Perkins, Barbara Boston, Virginia Ramsdell, Barbara Yorke, and Fred Wilson. The teacher is Althine Wyman.

JACOBS' GARAGE. Pictured are, from left to right: John Jacobs, Reginald Jacobs, Esther Miller, Charley Moore, Leslie Welch, Harold Hilton, Jr., and "Snyder" Hildreth.

HUTCHIN'S GARAGE was decorated for the celebration of the 300th anniversary of the Town of Wells in 1953. This garage began as a blacksmith shop in the 1840s.

VALERIE'S RESTAURANT before an addition was built on the left side of the building.

DANIEL NORTON DRIVING THE HORSE-DRAWN WATER TANK that was used to wet the dusty roads. This was a project of the Ogunquit Improvement Society.

THE DEDICATION OF THE VETERANS MONUMENT AND PARK. In August 1967 the monument was unveiled on the site that was formerly the location of the Dr. Gordon property.

POLICE CHIEF CECIL PERKINS, J. SCOTT SMART, AND EVERETT LORD. Jack Smart was the life of the community. He was famous for his Bloody Marys and his role as radio's "Fat Man." He is shown here with his friends at the fire station.

REGINALD JACOBS was chief of the Ogunquit Volunteer Fire Department for twenty-four years.

THIS 1883 READING STEAM PUMPER was given to the fire department by Hugh Ames for use at special events. Carroll Kemp is holding the reins while the stoker, a friend of Hugh Ames, stands at the rear.

THE LITTLEFIELD BLOCK IN THE 1940s. It was rebuilt after a fire destroyed the post office, the drugstore, the barbershop, and three apartments on December, 1934.

A RAGING FIRE AGAIN DAMAGED THE BUSINESS DISTRICT and destroyed most of the Littlefield Block on May 15, 1982.

THE DRUGSTORE WAS COMPLETELY DEMOLISHED. Summer visitors found the familiar streetscape being completely rebuilt when they arrived for the 1982 summer season.

THE BUILDINGS WERE COMPLETELY GUTTED by the fire which turned the business center into a disaster area.

THE OGUNQUIT VOLUNTEER FIRE DEPARTMENT was supported in its efforts by fire departments from the surrounding towns. They were unable to save the buildings that were already affected, but prevented the fire from spreading to other buildings.

JOHN NEILL'S EMPTY EASELS AT PERKINS COVE stand in silent tribute to the artist who occupied this spot for so many years.

Acknowledgments

Special thanks to Mary Hipple for the images that she made available to me, and to Charles West for providing high quality prints from less-than-perfect negatives. Thanks, also, to the Ogunquit Playhouse, the Ogunquit Public Library, the York Public Library, the Wagner Collection, Peter Moore, Everett Norton, Ruth Freeman, Sylvia Hutchins, Leonard Wyman, and Caroll Kemp.

A tip of the hat to Katie Rowe who generously shared her photo collection, her knowledge of Ogunquit, and her time. She helped me research pictures of questionable origin and rearranged her busy summer schedule to insure that I would meet publishing deadlines. She shared my goals for the book and made it possible for me to meet the standards that I had set for the publication.